Public Displays of Affection

Jim Leftwich

LBP

LUNA BISONTE PRODS

2023

Public Displays of Affection

Jim Leftwich

*While sitting beside a river -- or standing before the ocean,
or walking through a forest, or wandering in the desert –
are not sitting zazen, these activities do have similarities
to what John Cage referred to as quieting the mind. So the words that
are juxtaposed for reasons other than semantic are not intended to result
in absurdity, or comedy, or surrealism -- though some of that inevitably
comes into play. These juxtapositions are meant for the most part to be
engaged as quiet, tender, meditative encounters with what once was
called "something more deeply interfused".* – Jim Leftwich, June 2023

Cover photograph for *Public Displays of Affection*
by Sue Leftwich, San Simeon Bay, May 2023.
All other photographs by Jim Leftwich, Olympic Peninsula, 2022.

Thanks to the Public Libraries and the Librarians in Pahrump, NV,
Blythe, CA, Cambria, CA, Forks, WA, and Port Angeles, WA for the
use of their facilities in the preparation of the first rough draft of
this manuscript.

Thanks to Mark Young at Otoliths,
Marco Giovenale at slowforward,
and Dirk Vekekmans at Platformplee
for publishing some of these poems.

ISBN: 9781938521942
https://www.lulu.com/spotlight/lunabisonteprods

LUNA BISONTE PRODS
137 LELAND AVE
COLUMBUS OH 43214 USA

Table of Contents

Public Displays of Affection

You have a dog?
No.
Cat?
Yes.
You have a cat.
Yes.

_____

frigid bird wave loam looms
circular nose in the peach
no less below the music
than passing or missing
leaping wildflowers whistle
in our suits the doves are
a truckload of editions
leave the writhing to the
griffons the theological
pickleweed the moths
for months and months
looking for banjo math
in the magic country
lumen dining on daisies
just a few days left
of food found poems
and public displays
of affection

_____

Any fruits or vegetables?

4 avocados. 3 bulbs of garlic.
2 bananas. 1 tomatillo.
Ok. Where are you coming from?
Virginia.
Welcome to California.
Thank you.

———————————

oxalis Birdseed
caveat Vermifuge Bisects
Cuneiform chalice
beachcombing Cavalier
bodies & Doubloons
field mustard Gravy
raining Gravitas
elevation propaganda airy
windmill Rigor
Quivering weedless
ergo ergonomic ergot
eyebrows Dwindled frenetic
Afterimages Fandango
Alfalfa canal
almond poppy muffins
agribusiness asterisks
agog Gaping agape
Gobble Calzone Sinatra Toccata Coalition
Roasted corn & ginger tea
tomatillo rye Yarrow
toy hauler rubric Urbane
young cherry trees
indulged by Orbital hares
urinate pristine clubs depleted
azure lacewing

Copper monsters guarding
Fumaroles from Bambi
Lacerated worm science
Soggy as a map

until Yearly Understandings
tamarisk by tumbleweeds
Replete prismatic bran oration
esthetic teeming
tooth ringer moose hutch
Grist glistening tinsel
Havoc Goose Flinging
Northern hinge caboose
nasturtium turbulent
Moxibustion booster
brink of narrowing
milk-winged kings

Letteral imagination
Combing
Assembled realities

Orange ouch
leeching
ovenbirds lipstick Ouija
Invasive rain-streaked window shield
Oval sunflower
Over the
crouching cellophane

openly Pea protein
pianissimo Orchestrated
pink X-rays
Zodiac

Avocado Sweeping
dog Dodging Switchbacks
devil's cornfield
Afflatus
statistically impossible Festivities
diabolical Doodling
Sea salt Fungible
World Quietus
withholding garlic

encyclopedia
emitting aesthetics full of long stairs
wild and useless

Estuaries
forthcoming frothing meals & hierarchies
Epede Epede
never the gaseous word-fossils
that mask our helpless
spirals
Class C beehive
cat ebbs eventide

Sonorous partitions
Children
Of stagnant didacticism

Bermuda buttercup
banana
bulbs banter
dog berm
fecund mud
Sage butler
Snow-capped Shoes
and arrowweed

4

canned genius facilitates
the numerically senseless
watering the Arizona desert
to feed cattle in Saudi Arabia

Febrile
waggle Femur
dandelion
Ground squirrel Ermine
gaggle of
Loincloths

Russian thistle
dew point Oxalis Poppies
Octagonal Poems plural
ordinal
isthmus & walrus
indelible urinal cakes

hurts o'clock
bird-gap kitchen

yes scraggly & snaggle
Socks
ventriloquist
Rain rhythms on the roof
resting flocks of
Verdigris
vanitas
emergent Guesswork
Jests
finagle the Eggs
eucalyptus Raggedy
Desktop pests

Ziggurats & emergencies
variorum
sordid calculus
weekends Edible
Fewer Eternities Rainy

dedicated
one thing after another
Dabbled Dwindling
We Eat we eat
raindrips on the Windshield
Raw winding nibbled decal
The next version of
The next Cottonwood
verbs follow nouns
bench follows Batch
Fifth wheel Boat
That's the Pacific ocean
On the other side of
Those pine trees

Passage of Sidvig
zaum is a verb
Calculated
canine canasta
curvature
of lacunae
Nothingness
like interstellar space
teeming between
The letters

scrambled daggers
pointed by hand
at the unitary certainly
of language

this week our monthly doubt
the first armed algae of our
generation everything is
broken that has been
changed

this week the role of shoes
images of hats and nostrils
insomuch as the map pages
are unreadable illegible
desemantized & repetitive
all in all the watches are at
least an hour off in one way
or another design cannot
within the mind bend
emergent centers
backwards
before the architecture
of our metaphors
we are horrified
by the character
of charred wind
chanting collages
in the academy

heliocentric
havoc hachures
Monterey Pines chip seal
kilowatt ours
Juvenile Kilowatts
ursine illegible
defamiliarized ostrich
pink salmon Ocean
Municipal metaphors

hunch Munitions
haunch hence hinged
marsupial tensegrity

terse lava across
nonsyntactical
dirigibles

The book of
Contemporary
Suns

Baobab agglutinated
Right-handed dance

feral melts
corn on the cheese of time
a coin
acorn
mural felt horn
cheese windy drip
on the acorns of time

Towards snow now
Verbs & herbal gerbils
cull call dill

lemons Bubbling preamble
pensive & 'pataphysical

civic viewfinder baroque

Caveat bicycle Cave fish

Volcano per racket
per metrics in cheese

Ulterior lip pillow
incandescent Pulchritude
asymmetrical sandstorm
samovar aspergris
salmonella vault
auscultation ink
sod seme said
as was awash
weary same of periscope
way of the monetized cult
ersatz test tube radio
rewind wandering enigma
vouchsafe safety couch

automatic rice adorned
with paleolithic Beltane

cyborg aboard
iceberg Bagatelles

irregular failures
of posterior
questioning

gibberish beyond
temptation and
trumpeting thirsts

guts guts and
twists of the
knives and nerves

Pandemic inserted
In rational anatomy

obstinate & rotary
rotary also obstinate
exhaustive and sullen
ventilation

Formal desires
Within an economy
Of contexts
Yellow knife
sliced avocado
preferential legumes
He said
Is that a poem?
And I said yes.
And he said
How can you tell?
And I didn't
Say anything.
yellow spoon
red Withstanding
Rice mustache
emollient
rotisserie
safely Decidable
Sabbath-sulk
foodstuff Deductible
Dependent Schism
verisimilitude

fishing in place
Gestalt by the numbers

Copper suit asymmetrical
delta egg continuum
flagging Flock of
hauntological
goldfish Goldfinch Frock
hagiography
TypoKinetic energies

If I am writing a poem
A long poem
Sixty years long
Or longer
When I am writing a poem

I will let you know

Alternative and popular irregularities

obstruction
Inspection
Affection
occasion
tufted puffins

If Only lost
Like a
Marble or
hidden Mythologies
hidden Hierarchies
verbatim bending

Bending
To the beat

vouch bunched nonsuch
variously
non-committal
Branch
Approximate Foxglove Bunch
serene Dispersal
fixity Severance

Different feathers
Different feet

rhododendron & crepe myrtle
Weeping turtle dendrites
Epoch Reaping roadhouse

we Enigma
effortful

Withholding
as Sunken
Dirt glyph forsaken
Hieroglyph
forgotten Herein
Hurtful
handful
grotto of fins
fennel with diamonds
how in the world
given forth has
dirt Foggy fingers

as it Goes
Good
Yes
The best one yet

audio parachute qualia
Generosity treatment

Ear Ear of the Rib
rubs against the Wings
Didactic poetry
cinema cinders
Flux of Variations
car pox Vaccine
dazzling lungs
linger over
lunch
dust of Silence
dirt such Further
earlobe of Ribcage
enigma of Wings
Rubs them the wrong way
Verified fruition
did I tell you?
feather not
The Furry Dirt

Uselessly out of
Urgent lingering
If Only
Popular audio
Afloat
On bitter espresso
once in Place
Alongside the Open

Road kinnikinnick
kilometers of Lump

inner Loop Oleander
Outer pool eye
Carrot bystander
loom Of my mule

Myrtlewood carving
mouse stash
burstnorm music upper
limit, remember?

nicely panicked
Meanders Birds norm
noetic marbleized
letteral lemniscate lambent
lupine aquatic aquiline
hyena grouse hydrated sage
granted engaged gyrations
goose quill penetrant
byline gastric
feline
fertilized

Resin
resonant
resurgent

velocity
clearcuts
vacuity
beyond the

14

Velcro
bilateral
foregrounding
Greenwashed
revolt
half Elliptical

foundational Residue
ground cover
Repurposed

The Hoh River
Swollen
With snowmelt

rush and rye Yet Tapestry
undersurface Tremors serrate
unguent glue Tumescent
Whiteleaf Manzanita
bobbing lobed
Hasten the Calvary
Rooster through the Tinsel
Robbery in the Brushfields

Troubling Routines --
how Real are the Reals?
how about Real
Life road Training?

how The Hoh
River appears
Reins instead
Re7 real teal

Reinsinuated
By glacial snow
Melting flowers

corsage and fragrant
prescience
in a fallow suitcase
tempest Emergent
germane Earnest Rebuttal
egg Eldritch Rhizome
Verifiable Dirt Visage
Doppler feathered war chest
We Festoon & detune
Cinematic cinder cones
discourse Clinamen
desemantized Veracity

bygone ontological
Fragments of creativity
Bastions of glacial flour
Maidenhair Spleenwort
Harebell
Mountain Bog Gentian
flowering triangular discus
Hairless Sunrise
Fear of Heat Domes
Do Not Think of a Poem
Read against the givens
Reading as a form of generosity
before the Fronds Golden
glistening lists
By now at least
the sonic piedmont mask
of the astronaut's
infinite torso

thuds merciless Methods and
Knots materials Notwithstanding
mutagens and
Kilometers Jettisoned
kettle of wishes
lukewarm Keening loments
Louisiana Hot Crawfish Sauce
looking Over my shoulder
pennies logic anxious subculture
Just another pelargonium
Open Octagon Influx
placards swarming
peeping moments inscape
Potentiometers in Open series
people get ready they
Called it Warrior
Music
Oil on the Line
In track as coming
Let the becoming be

Illicit Lastingness logistics
Jobber menthol behind Benthic
Mumbling Behind Nothingness
Mangling hindsight matchbox monetized
brunch of the neologisms
Magnetized nihilist Fennel
Humbled hangnail hunches

filch hitch
forth glitch Hilt folkloric Hunch
forwarding
Gaps Hatch

fetch
hutch Fastness
Gasp Hence
grasping first Hooch
translocal birthday collective
horse trance

hat banished
clambering things ladder To
do unspoken firebrands
purge euphemism

hemming Thimble Rethinking
recasting Hasten
remnants remake slant
telepathic antimony
to the tilt

finishing hostel
furbished & refurbished
homestead retrofitted
Reengineered
edpedpe
deadened Endings

criticality
eucalyptus seaweed
comprised of
erasures
caloric epigram
stairs carpenter monk
seal unleashed

all-star alienation
fatal anthropocentric
for the love of the hell of it god
a floating pocket of
autonomy fortune digger
arrhythmic
garbage bag waggle tagged
gag bag wag tag sag lag
ancestral nebulae
gastric albedo
As far as we know
gaps hatch

sampling dialectical plunging
frenzied narratives
Latitude canola Dimensions mirroring
folded and refolded and unfolded
shadowy checkerboards
of airplane horizons
viral X-ray war machines
Axiom Volute pining corpus sensorium
conceptual scrum
Vibratory blue canoe numes
Blighting Mythopoeic the
blue rose the noctilucent Mirror
Fleet Van Heart
mostly Levitating Clocks & Vouched
Nexus nuanced numen
Mutagenic memento Mori
burnt Nova veil cement mini humidifier
verboten cobra snake for a necktie
Box Cars rolling in reverse
Anonymous portals to Economic Viruses
mountainous Non fungible
Volcano Catapults

comb moral Voice

Camel on the Run
toxic coal ash voucher
cavernous curvaceous variable
bulbs venturing across a
border Navigating
Barn buffers Biggest
gigabytes & firewalls
hurling goats for charity
How much Time do we have?
Years & years times years
Years Utterly

utile in situ undertow
inexpensive outwardly
immersive Unburdened
Imbricate Ombudsman
Immutability Occidental
Intrusive Offensive five
olive inclusive pensive
Toehold cowardly U-turn

infrathin croquet cul
de sac pitched bottles
knit kites knife
kitchen knife knots
longing from being
Knit kitchen kites
Lungs birthing prattle
lozenge oval zen

Main meant mind
moot mute mood
music mind mere
make
socio-environmental weekly

enigma rebuttals
we are maps of the ricochet
emptying
exemplary enthusiasts
deconstructed deeds & constructs
deem of Emissions
dreams of
Remissions and Emulsions
eatery we landfills
ectoplasm the goofy
Creeps the creepy Goofs
Circus emitting Caucus
Consensus to the sea

as shriveled pulsars
dwindle bird dogs
Apostolic suitors
dabble behind
flags aboard windmills
who Quibble
destitute Quirks
for Quisling perks &
Quixotic Intuitions

roosting roister
Winterized
towards Waste rock and
tailings
Wet cosm
Warmly Failing
schizocarp For Two
Squid guild Dancing
grunions giant goldfish
Dolphins & Sharks
Diploid minnows
harsh Deflections of
Deep sea fictions

between Boundaries woven
common augmented Beckoning
cosmos because Cosmetic
neologisms coined hordes
bent scalable Nous
Slab knob spruce seduction
blot Mapping Brute norms
meant mounds movement
bottom Naught Meeting
Gossamer gauze goetic
holographic Gourds
hence Fallible Gooseneck
hobbled nabob retention

He were feet

brunt of the
leg up
understated

invisible events
resize
durational echoes

Barbecued & Biblical & Noetic
Mere as rib
ghastly
Most of the time
Ghostly Cadillac
Far has lasting

Hold on tighteners
Twin ere Repulsion
Task to be
redundant Tastes
even toes Two we ochre
else abundant
elsewhere abdicated
were quietly Dehiscent
we quickly behind
Everywhere culmination
adz commodified
furze reified
Cozy module
very cozy vacancy
causal vox coffee Vaccine
By the time you see this
Cairn Barn Corn
ventral Bioluminescent
flocculant culinary
fragrant Granite
How do they do it?
They're going out of business

Trembling lingers lungs
triplicate lunge Your
trilobite my lunch break
tulips Under primate
yearning unilaterally
unbreakable acetates

o ponds IOU
Petrochemical
us legume Yet

Who do you louver who Lapse
enunciated wherewithal
volunteers Defenestrated
Verities heavyweight lifted
Like Deracinated Ballast

---

we are at our core non-progressive
contemporary bastions of degrowth
before the magical institutions
with their shoestrings and
their soiled parachutes
we are here to solve
choices of the
strongest importance

Left spoon the
darkened half
For Socialist paces
punctual claw of
gravity quarterly
Reports gravy snake
snack slack Warts
westerly retorts
tangerine Restitution
trampolines Tart
Yearly Torts
Yesterday

upaya ulcerated coral loops
ozone implants imploding
Oceanic Periscope pirates

of Post capitalist
Lotus Yoyo Osage
totipotence Unbeknownst
triune wrench Watch

cardiovascular Vagaries
Oxygenate bivouac crumbs
Many Crumbling Mary
None ambushing neon
Backsliding Volatile segue
disengaged chronology
Complex daily lungs
Eat solo new & vast
bitternut Nodules
coaxing oaken
gluten daemonic
fitting Glut Hachures
Jabbering Krill
Hegemonic juke
Laryngitis solar
Array awry awake
let them eat snake

firmament roaming
sacred delta map
Groveling prescient
Heroic Blue Heron
buffet scarred by
cola non rafa green
barista Ricotta
vacuum Glum
Verge webbed moat
gyre Tuning
backhand Helium
cypress grove

Hub of mercurial
no middle way
Yearn of the Norms
Unbending Meanders
unblemished massively
unending instead

Objects grocery
Essential orange
Fob lorry or jets
please Lanky
Anklets

Plug nickels on the
dune Gold feathers
In a fist Variable
mandala Kindling
Knuckled bayou
Mingling dugouts
Yet Fire on the
Leather grist Garbled

ephemeral carafe
who invincible
Skin
dreadful Elastic
wuthering

seductive finagler
convokes
Continuous Xylem
vomiting Duplex Curmudgeon
dependably cantankerous
consecutively

26

eking remonstrance
revoked Turquoise
Rainbow bonnet
Sinking

Trilogy tabby
bat flying fruit
boy barley homily
toy trumpet solidly
annoy urn alloy
busy sycamore
by iodine cat
inverting the eye

involuntary oatmeal lottery
scribbled the present as a
Public dialogue provoking
one up on the letdown

pristine muck lorn
looming
at shadow's edge

Messy mossy lessening
Us lessons guesses
tossed jobber meringue
by gusts of lust
resurgent by bursts of
Dust insurgent
Detergent
jocularity parity
Rarity profundity Fanity
gists and pithy gristle
Vested atoll

skillful Festering
squirrel debate
destiny televised
folding Gunk
interrogates the
surface of the text
derogatory dates
guest sunken
Doldrums Savant
Gamut cogs and
clogs Drumming
Slug dagger Gut
fiend of demure
Silence Fiction
blessed vocables
drag fractional
reserve dragons
victorious and
dire from the
River in their Veins

quadrangular Escargot
quitters never Fake
early rivers
of the Floating Whirls

ravine Vocative caving
dictionaries fence Gnoseological
ravages Tumbling tumbling
rotary tarmac penury
Gaming the systemic
distribution chain links
for the Gold of Love
for the duration
tantamount to dinner
Just so is How it Happens

kilter Ubiquity Yestereve
invokes
oily salvaged outskirts
prevailing from
Sublimated
cicada lake sutra
yestermorn Tantric
ravens and egrets

Democratic
vocalizations desalinate
the Silver vase

———————————

communal variations on
wavicles in a Vitrine
with or without Beyondsense

Eggs hasten
Authentically Universal
Wastewater
westerly Uncannily
wistful Undaunted
East of instinct
Eggplant inner Rasputin
overtly Tsarist
pointed leaves Tainted
putty Twister
poultry Taciturn
oxidative mind streaks
King of Knaves
disjunct Jarring
harvest safeguard Heaviest

ashen basalt Groundcover
Gas cookies messengers
Supplies walnuts gas
Atlas Canadian Geese
saltier High School lunch
Room memories of
horse cheese Skeletons
fingernails honeybees
wind chains
Nocturnal bolting
Eggs batten

bad poem bald poem braided
poem mad poem clad poem
clay poem play poem praying
poem radiant poem dented
scratch and dent demented
syntax without representation
bad poem no chewing on the
sofa no pissing on the carpet

so Be it everhereafter
crisp sweet weasels
of the secret forest
caveat uncalled vitriol
Against the Translucent
Method of condensation
in Expressionist Asemia
By way of Citrine Xanadu
my truth is the best truth
The piano sun moisture
of Liberation is also an
axiomatic mixological
X-ray due vessels limited
Tune and scroll could go
On like this forever

doom Jump
doom Jump
doom Leap
Fail Leap fill
Public Libraries
Full foil fuel
leap Jump
feel far fur
For free fins
root Oak
Tree fish
Loom Loom

Typographic Tentatively
inscrutable passage Timely
Parrotfish set fires
real long eels remembering
Encyclopedic Urging
My questions Quickly
quantitative Talisman
We are sage typist swordfish
Under the Eternal Sky
Until the Internal Sky
Unknown maybe useful
emptiness of the
Unending
splotches
Against
a Terminal Sky

Gaps
convinced
Designs written in rice
Sky settled sitting
food dancing singers

fitting rife contaminates
abrasion
auscultation

as if away always again

said agile algorithms singly
Few mingled sesame flavors
Fletch them on the fives
we are Empty but we have
The cool whip

Effortful Fortitude
efforts who Fortified

fire Relives Emanation
communal flaws
depauperate roadside flyways
Rescind Free expression
Eventuate Vacuums
deranged

arbitrary Sulfurous
As the House of Salad
Delineate ferrous
Adrenalized
Affronts to Linearity

expropriate fizzles Extinguisher
Excommunicated nurse trees
Temenos fuzzy infrastructure
Unbecoming irredentist precipitation
postdated depleted snowpack

let the letters lust
let the Leaflets lunch
leaf lunch letters list

Make the most
Of this much

a few watchmakers create sounds
to be urgently modern reclamation
laminated & lacerated as we
transition from minerals to
interior mammals
roaming these roads their copper
miles burdened by permanent
windlass arsenic
the flaming collapse
the sea of time
cultures forever sensitive
to the consequences
of their inaction

Laundry facade consumes
Private chowder behind
The Comedy Country
Club verging on Ever
River fever emerging
Biocrusts flammable
Vibrancy branching
dreadnought ultraviolet
demigod plotless
A fifth of fifth and a half

turncoats cite cuts
timeless oysters incubate
cyanobacteria unbuttoned
orality unscented
patchwork instant composition
pummeled indefinitely
ordinarily Unfurling
If you Hey
if You Uh
Our lips quip quit
Slip opt Pause
utmost incipient laundering
Yet
Nimble movies
hirsute
Manichean
haggle groin Mantra
history forever nearby
Real-time composing
Neverending oeuvres
hourly reports
everything Behind
Here and the Eightball
be the Genius Germ Genus
cultivation
vocables walking on wafers
Variables of the Human Heart
we Call and respond
To the qubits Futures

Flex driven Ripples
team players stretched foreseen
yantra Tylenol canola

My other openness is an
improvisational epistemology
is this how poems

are written
Yes
Only out West
On Sundays
denounces dynamic
debris of denunciation
Always and Everywhere
upper limit Outside
how unreachable is
Proportional Ownership
Of the Love poem
Urgent Jumping Yelping
harrumphing rumpled
juvenile hint of Miracles

haggard greatly Hollow
ragged and Gallant
ah debunked blinkers
Alterity junket
Astral juice Adjudicated

We nurseries Whet
due Eruptions
irreverent Ruptures
Testimonial
overconsumption
Voynich
Cereal bellicose
Causes believable

neural larvae
visitations Bequeathed
two-headed dog force Humbly
Gravitational fungus
Breathless content curves
godzillions of hair triggers

a greasy Trombone
resonates

extraordinary Vectors
dysraphic
vegetable Factoid
Developmental
detour corridors
fractal Deep
images grown swiftly
Hectares
Holographic Gloaming
four fables flop
longer than you think

Perpetually
oil stained perplexed
inundations presumably
Blue years abstain

mannequin Neighbors Beyond
moon landing thrives
Lesser Lasso Lossless destiny
kitchen Knife barren
famously futurist anonymity

wherein were squashed
Square
as an arribada
zigzag
through the waves

Snoozing Stereotypes

Were Estimated
egg muffin Escutcheon
raphesemic
said sod Surveying
Acrobatic or
atomic
astronauts Rot gut
aromatic nozzles
atypical Rusting Teflon

————————

discuss less popular debt
ceilings under their grow
lights why hammer the
inspired texture tubes
only meandering the
servile toothpaste not
all flavors of language
are are nonsense or
pure jelly the breakfast
of livestock releasing
greenhouse fertilizers
deep into the produced
water clearer in the
morning than ever before

excavated
molted numinous
unmoored

intuitive Umbilical
Only In Opposition
portents

of
light
Luminous
Lacerated
killjoy
how many Jurisprudent
modernity Quibbling
equality wants to know
we Want to see
we Quivering quicksilver
Want to be
raiment
Pew accrue
raids upon the garments

as spores Disperse
arid syncretic Dada
amid Algae
doodles Assume

Zazzle Zoom

As if
The God of Fire
Has two
Wives

X-ay coverlet
Exquisitely
unpersuasive
Barbarian Rudiments
Flavorless &
quiescent

My authority Garment

Questioned In two
Rose Gnostic
Caustic flows
As the crow flies
want To have
want to give
rose Yes Even
yes symbolist
lest embolism
Vested schism
prismatic nest
Best of seven
Heaven knows
A throw of the Dice
Useless Diaspora
upstairs no
refunds from
The fire sale

Yippee Plenty Yatch
plenty Nothingness
indeterminate
mosses Diametrically
Disbursed
Desemantized
jawn
junior semiotics
jars of Remedial
urgency
help Potato kelp
lichen yam Plurality
Pyre
Pistil Yap
pestle Yeti
Telesterion
What we want

Coevality
sliding scale of Vitality
dust on the pivotal Disk
evaporates

carburetor exile
maximum comeuppance
More than a little
can the music play
Calming anxiety
Kiosk of Longing
glass of Loss
kiosk of delinquent Years
Sequestration
Useless light of Yearning
glut of Tardigrades Yet request
teeming Eupsychic Umbrellas
Units if next
issues of use
slouched infinities
out in out in
our picnic table
our inside
useful ingots
utility bill
our electricity
our inner usefulness
out of invoices
use our insight
unused excess

textbook mixtures
photovoltaic
default Vestigial
vault doorless

Toilet vestibule
advances Distraught

several tedium
average Delirium
voltage Carrion

Degrowth Effectively
Extremities
are what we
asyntactic
apron map edging
meanwhile
bigger
Are air arc and
aim age
era
rare
as pigs
flying hen's
teeth napkin
fireflies
anthropomorphic
agile in a
golden age of
poetry
a gust of pairs
asparagus
gusts a pair of
gusts
Agrarian

a tablecloth
a tablespoon
gathered at the

What we
Want to do

Eat
Even
Ein Sof
Fiction is a façade
Epoch
feelings of being Eaten
Epic Fallout

Encouraged growing mountains
suppressed maverick pretexts
longitude along an upgrade
Possible openness
Open possibilities

thriving down the
Vortex
economic theories Jonquil
boutiques
mysterious Localities

now unlike poems
time hosting Poetry
Would
style Cultural lapse
diary epicenter

verbatim nuclear
first felt
Writing thickens
Lung

_____

solitary lacunae coalition
attached by magnetic bones

ennui chiasmus literature
variable as a scheme

Moon moss mesh mush mash
hewn Mown moan hone horse
horn cairn mane name harsh
mood mess nest push gash
told toed toad tolled tune floss

smoldering anthills escape recreational
signifiers by gruesome emotional climate
changeling within moments of repertory
clamor close proxy fleas camphor and
clarion stocks cliffs one side of the
wandering mountains experiential
waiting rooms yellowed booste
countdown out by the lake where
it is raining books

temblor Trident
Vichyssoise
coarsely Bacteria
cones vibrant
blemish

Childhood tantrums pantomime
Laborious tsunami

bracts Cottonwood Varicose
Utility lightning
perk ravel pickle ash lake
if painting a flat rock
Pointed as a fact
as shrubs
seabird guano asbestos
as sticky
salt on the pork
as futile hovel fainting
shrivels drier
annointed with rubber
wherein we
were whereas
roadside we
visited the Pacific Ocean
at dawn
bolster and sequester
better & Bigger
grovels like a fuse
gabled fish ends
touched by fingertips
the tips of the
gristle and guts

or drooping
rocking
chair

one at a time
You got the food
You got the flivver
Working overtime
Free five for a dime
piccolo whale hymns

screaming conversation
you got the fire escape
rewind the Wind
Reinsinuated
ersatz the moon
rigor motorized
snafu on the side
side hassle on the fins
Digging like a Soup
fire on the Dim
Dimmer Switchback
vermiform
frothing at the Grins
flugelhorns & Fustian
how many more ears
Da srim ce golf
gulf of Gulf of Forms
holstein Tyro Kine

lateral Intuitions
oblong lacerations
optimized

Indeterminate Olio
Moist
hymnal Musk
What do you think
He is thinking?
verbs of Broken
Mustard
veal buttonless nodules
vintage
noodles calibrated
Boxcar caliper Fissured
Bottom of the Heat

so Ditches
for Shiny
Dilate the fictions
epoxy hue
remedial Wrinkles
Endemic Remedies
we Etch forth
emptier and fluffy

We
arc Serpentine
Digits fandango
Hairy gloom
fatalistic Hearsay
He
handcrafted
giraffe fumes
fundamentally
hopeful
guesswork fixated
hydraulic
did you Figure
It out?
ash Gothic
Godzillions
amortized
Germ wargames
Ending on a
Sour sound
Each river
Unlike every
Other River
In real time
Written
Dawn
corridor axial
Viscosity

creampuffed
Axles Viscous
dogwood
dirtier Soil
defeatless Futures
emptying the Rivers
echoing Wristwatch
Rewinding the wind
Verily
doom frothing
Forward through
This Door

Undersides Linchpin outer
immaterial margins
left Of the Peels
orbiting our inner
Refusal of the
Psithurian Call
Left Of the Sleep
knit Lacks abound

Loose Leaflets Opening
Into an Outside
locomotive Ounces
Musicality of the
meteors & their craters
bristled muscular nodding
Mirrored Branchlets
nocturnal masking
looks loot looming loops
liminal catnip scratching

hollower men than
gallop swallowing

black garlic
gaseous nebula of
foothills foot
loose footing

Rounded to
rodeo ready
round
up the bend

varies according to
ventriloquist
by antioxidants the
Vulgar
beef Gear
flips him
on his Ear

for this Reading
given the flowing river
Rotten Twigs
rhythm Triangular
cultural utility
Knife The
upright piano
Tuner
beat & beat less
History is like that
Return To the
Right Behind
The Red Schoolhouse
history is Read
how many
brokered Readings

Then their
Leveraged Interpretations
held To the allicin
tight endings and
Eternally
germane Errors
Return of the Sender
eggs on Every Ridge
Vocalized Diamonds
The Very Few
Dancing
In the streaks

We Forehead Canyons
discovery Coddled Vast

Nothing left but cockroaches
Eating money
Flexible gasket control
Bitcoin garbled
Hedonist Golfing fascists
divided by Hopeless change
In Job Mountain were food
Agents insecure and
Floundering Homeward
Menace chronic chaos Threat
Rigged and more Rigged
by Famous Goons
grinning in my face once
Bitten twice two steps
Shy of the treasure

———————

sulking breath movements engineer
unexamined blueprints already the
tentative behemoth of planetary
pathos and restlessness

segue articulate realities
& unofficially inarticulate
realities officially rational
non sequiturs thank you

legitimate salvific perfection
in the tempo of realized peace

Alembic Hydration
Alkahest Astringent
utilitarian Energies
insistent Emerging Rituals
Or Rigorous
obstinate Timidity
perk Yearning peaks
Meaning fuel Mist series
cluster Management microbial
Nexus Normalized
Crux of the Norm

Zebras with cows
In pastures
Below the castle
Fallacy of Azure
horizontal ginger
Stranger gerunds

Jangling angels
Jingle angular
dangling Kites

flaming gelatin
Ginger Lungfish
gangly kittens
Blameless bells

Evidently a genetic tirade catalog
Confronted by blemished research

We barnacle
built host structure
through four ramps
banana
to be decided later
by the time we
tabulate the
tabby cat
through a boneset
Equitably
Vitamins
ravel earshot
vanity of the lamps
resuscitate
In banter

We Curlicue
counterclockwise

Might grow toes
And spread
Bread in the sunlight

Clots We wavering
closest circuit
when meandering

Volumetric
extract versus
thermal velocity
redacted

tannins non-anti
Thunderstorms namelessly
Yellowed

Year-round miraculous
enzymes & bear
Spray unanimously
Mirage of the New
urbane sour paper
unbroken Skeptical
sugar

inside the squared circle
pickle
terrain
in stride in stride
Peppery periphery
inherent patterns
leathery porridge
unguent
Unbent
Unwinding in Onions
Units

the Retina of History
Yam festivities Underscored
Roundabout Turnout
Yesterday is Postscript
rest on our
Edible Laurels

why quiz we Each
wrong realization of
The right Turn
riot Tern Yatch
turn Yatch U-turn
styptic stick urn
Earn your own
Onions
Yatch

in the pollination quadrant
The Oil sticks to itself
Like blood
In a family of Glues

In the potassium Incinerator
clot ubiquitous Yearlings
titanium over the Teapot the
Epic "we" encumbered with
Queries who and why they
Read and reread the Unread
Earthlings reach for the sky
Try this at home Yearnings
Unencumbered by any Plot

impoxximate orchid
Proximal lupine Or
pyroclastic roses
Imitation liquidity
ulterior Options
cut inks
insidious Oils
My blue Oranges
inky
ohm lapis

lyrical Upstart
osage green
clutch Vacuum
Burgeons

Cooked Voyaging cult Bark
chemical Visigoths
Glossy
degrees flat
gremlin Fiddleheads
growing in the
Dark Forests
goiter nor Gatlin
Dribbling nouns
From Dungeon to gallows
differential Fenugreek
Gallic acids
Gamblers on the run
Darkly through glass Woods & Forests
winter protein Emergencies
Raw & Rank we
recall the weekly
Ashes to ashen dust to dusk
ash on a glass sparkling
alembic trickery area
right riot as rain
Are you reaching
For your revolver?

reinsinuated in an
Asyntactic whorl
Vertical invaders
Inflect in fact epede
an epistemic injustice
who swimmingly
In a raw lake
roar our gently boat

wai try ingmar
Waiting For----
asemantic wiggle room
at the Raw Luck Casino
Raw racket
are we willing and
able to go on?

Dare to Forget the
dust swordferns Dare to Forget the
vagaries of the anarchic kaleidoscope
Dare to Forget the
vagaries of the fastidious Bassoon
downpours ballroom
downtrodden barroom Dust
becomes
Belief Cause
becomes the Curse
vagaries of the Noodling Balloons

Bombastic brooms
moreover Barometric
molecular
brimming nihilist morse code
The New integral gas
And pink motif since
Tradition
Brokered No Medium
brilliance nor
Salmonberry Milking
Matriculated
Morticians
by the night of the Moon
Beneath the Full Noon night
mythic spikes test
soaking recidivist
disengaged sulks

reformed inferno
Reddish shipping
decibels of
Shrill Belief

Senior reddened
Tartar sauce
split-fingered &
Garrulous

dogs for gods Forever
gas second with new
song together of
pieces studio
forfending betwixt
Disturbed vanguards
Second song pieces
Denial of Coevalness
Forever within new
Wicks flickering
From Dust
To Dusk

rim ennui rudiment
weak Flimflam
oceanic mentation
rim ennui largesse
heretical magic
remnants as we speak

———————

Spring 2023
West Coast
USA

NO WRONG NOTES

In The Parking Lot At Willie's Laundromat

His Sky Blue Shoes

Heirlooms hijacked by heresy

Samson and Delilah

No Wrong Notes

Rotting Gnats the Poem

Yippee Pie Sky Day

Garbling the Genes

In The Parking Lot At Willie's Laundromat

Verbs eat the hammers
Eat the hammers
beat the hamstrings
Retreat the string quartet
Hammer the violins
Trimming why Hammock
Under the humming stars
Joy be the hummingbird

yearlong
unbeknownst
Quips quick trips
Put it Up
Inner Under
kiwi Your Trumpet
jumping horse boat
trumpetung sly jangly Teeth
horse house
house hopping
hopping horse
how Gritting the Funk horse
Funk Gritting a house
Gritting as it hops

For Dogs Forget
For Dogs & Dogs

As
As a
does
does
sad as a deer
does

Even if Quit Who
Quit Even Who
Even Who
Even Who Requisite
Required Eventually
ever true
retired
tried and tired

Yet muddlehaven
Nor bulb syringe
Noggin tomatillo
Noggin

vanity of banana olive
branch managers in bunches
Their shoes are worn out
Inflammable
Scribble on a cardboard box
Nobodaddy nibbling
Omega-3 protein fish
Big Fish Popdaddy Upanishads
Your Underbrush Is Nodding
Your understory is fleeing
With all of its pants
On Fire

loopid onionoid

poinint pointeded

Off-pudding
Oft-putting

ununder

if you if

Lilting Opines Preying Osprey
Scorpion upon
upon its own onion
Younger than Us now
ulterior motif inflations

Did
go forth doing
bidding
coaxing the
crisper waxing
xylophones chromatic vomiting
A pox of zen & zinc
Upon your curse
chromatic zaum waxing gibbous
Upon your 3-bean salad

Said ha Said Da
Eating with the
Wrong side of the
Fork
Eating your own toes
Taking out the trash
Talking amongst
Your multitude
Of selves

His Sky Blue Shoes

Vacancies
Vacate balloons
north of attention
backsliding away
from the Birdsongs
from the dance
from the graveyard the
graveyard training manual
ringing in the bears
true are the headless

yet useless
yet uselessly
uselessly open
& uselessly lyrical
Lyrical open nests
inchworm piano
inching bodies
thunder on the ocean
His Sky blue boots
Are yellow
Yellow Timing Belt Teeth
Teeming as they run
we have the fives
we want the whirling sand dervish
we would do anything
Not quite
Yellow as a quilt of quips
Quit man alive
Halving on the Fives

BoX of DoGs

Femur as they come
Gene splice on the dime

grinning in Your Face
gRinNing
In YOUR FACE
hog-tithed for hello
no Higher God than

mirror in the bathtub
Hymn Humming Ham

monkey pox hopscotch
July therefore
unless gravy blue
king knuckles uncle
kinder & gentler underhand
kinks of just intoned ice
locks loop
July knuckles lazy glue
July knuckles uncle antlers
Hinge and hinge
Of jockstrap soup

Fiddleheads Geranium
Dabbling Agrarian
Somnambulant Doodles
as closely reading
Is catnip

chicken
vernacular brimming
with Golfing Fascists

fit to try Tiresias
Box of Dogs
His sky blue
Boots are
Yellow
is up is on the once

is on the pomegranate
paper mill is on
Spruce river road
By once to try the
toy redwood tree awhile
Forever chemical witness

gabbro gambit ghoats
Forgotten Hoagies of ghost
Ghost Hamburgers helpless
fish waltzing toward king
four mad eye sun
eights ilk silken milk
By pulp avocado ear
Vultures rose fern reeking
environmental protection
agency picnic tablet
Ventures grumbling wings

Imbricate and Opening

filtration gizmo floating
disposable footprint
garbage garage cabbage
paper baggage
straight-line winds
bistro brusque gaping
syllabus in retreat

Nature is made of non-writing.
Drag erasing it run-on. Sentences.
The Maillard Reaction.
The totipotency of organic non-writing.

Hirsute shoebox bullies
hydrated rocket
coffee fragments
yet toenails
morphological verify
unrealistic minerals
mirroring eupsychic jonquils

muscular prosodic misadventures
June Bugs July Bags Big August
Jekyele jewelrhymes rimming
juicers corkscrew liminality

Work jumping lumps
Potential inquiries
limping jumps
notched slender
horizons twisting
oily protein synthesis
imbricate ornithologist

if no other poetics

unintelligible inquiries choired
crudites yucca monsoonal
composed yucca compromised
Compost Yucca Tropical
Undecidable Eggs evangelize
By cry dry eye fry gyre lye my
Pie rye sigh tyro vie why
with the lightwind
in my core
Queried Who dye
quicken those who dire
In an undersea fire
the emptiness between
my atoms is filled with
interstellar space

during contrary artifice
salmonberry eulogy withstanding
wholesome somatic attic
requisite wayfaring
emblematic dolmades
frequencies frenetic
decalcomania Coastal wasp's
nest plateau
durable Fevers trombone
gardening clinical hexagons
daffodils febrile
Verisimilitude studious
floor dwelling bluebirds Foul
dishtowel bedraggled
flattened downbursts
decidable frontiers
Books employees hooligans
The greening of Venus

The neocortical 5
Billion
Barrels
nota Bene
Quarterly Reports
not a HinGe
Jug band hinge aid
Mutual jumpstart
Gathering froths Healing
gadfly yearling
Changeling riveTing
roulette cyclone
rust putty Tilting Yesterdays
unctuous lip service
Yellowed like a pUrpLe mOOn

objective pLastic fLOtation lozenge
periodic viewpoint decay
projected interpretive Onionskin
unfolds chronons & calories
Teeming bicycle Yesman
eidolon radishes Tubular
decentralized salal Door Farming
food Demonized monetized
grinning Quonset whistlers
roaming mung bean
eidetic whittling Tortoise
gamelan adynaton ecstasis
readying the celestial
haecceity machine
Rejection Galvanized
strolls reHabilitated
Retrofitted Entropy
Ersatz Reminisce
teeming few
and far between

boom bam bim bum beem
doom dam dim dump deem
loom lam lim lump leem
moom mam mim mum meem
toom tam tim tum teem
zoom zam zim zum zeem
boom dam limp mum teem
beem dump limn maim zoom

Unfolding Clockwise
Variable conjunctures
noises nonviolent
brackish concave
vacuum cauliflower

Zoo Clock PoX Zoo Clock PoX
zoom counterclockwise pox
variations conjecture pox

Brackish consensual
Navigation Backwards
Biodegradable karma
Hummingbird Ghoat
Ghoat Fungible hiding
in the grass snake
eggs abject snake

Intentional lizard habits
Imbricate and Opening

Heirlooms hijacked by heresy

variations Rabbitual
Vortical rooming
birthday of the
thumbnail tornado

horizontal roaming
turpentine altitude
tortoise eyebrow
yortle through the
nose until the End

green hurdles mustard
jogging paves the beach
flaws ajar yodmyrtle

your subjective
crepe myrtles
against the mud

by up up by gone

ditch in the head

the fine five first

stand and sand

figure of speach

the spinach register

got hot jot lot

rat rut cat cut rot cot

gage gigo gu

ragged quietude

quickly rite quick &&
yourself squawking
yourself in selves
quiver yourself
question yourself
quaking Pando
yesterday's squiggles
ubiquitous wonder
underculture
eat with intuition
risen & shin
twin bubbles baking
otic
pyramidal

griffonage
acts of griffonage
asemous haunts of griffonage
jotting it down like a griffon
Gryphon
kinship futile griffin
loosely
loosening
footwriting
jalapeno of the dogs
historiography
asemantic gambling

zoological soy voltage

zoot zawn Sam

xeric nightness

my verbs insist
my verbs inside
my verbs instead

noxious barricade
razzles barrier
noxious drizzling
forever noxious baubles
vortex dazzles between
drops raining
chemical drips
silent slipstream

who
how when
what what
why where
who
howlever sobeit
edenic pomology
under
due until
dew point drops
falling rocks watch
for fallen rocks
oily road
oceanic tondo
open the
unbroken
windows

filled with

isomers
of lyric
Rimbaud
is open to
a longing
& a loss

limping liminal Lump
the kiss of Desk
mishearing is
an art

nor none at noon
neither nothing
in the night

broom on the wind
before the sun
valley of the vowels
ready to startle the day
credible computations
chromatic crucible In C
caveat compelling
egret eating the snowy fog

verbal visitations
vocable variations
gaffe tubulin within
and without non-writing
dog numerals point blank
hurrier hurrier
permanently fleeting informatics
temporary seconds
in a jiffy of a hurry

yesless tranquility surrounds
Our moribund blogs
up to no food
pulse & impulse
optimal & pituitary

gusts of history jackknife

heirlooms hijacked by heresy

error fur
errant fury
ersatz fairies
was plural
during
simplex
furthermore
decomposed
structuralist
fanfare

kiln luxurious
jackal slurred
libations
verbena
nevermore

backslider's
non-denominational
bitterroot navigation
monsoonal barrister
buckdancing
diphthongs
duplicity of the gods
glib gibberish

gnawing at their
rowboat

error of their waves

efforted furthering

via diametrical detours

verbatim timing

fog soggy
blogs froggy
hog noggin

Tomatillo on the squirrel

yes juts
us yes jilts
yes us
us yes
us
our us is
jolts yes

pig raffle 6
a ruffled pig

proof of the getting

bootstraps
all by themselves

dollhouse bootlegging
eyebrows
her highness
eh etching the wretch
tidal mythologies of
holy water on the
wafer / watery holes

the why
but why
why and
eye why
rye why
gristle
gizzard
trigonometry
try sly
tow hasty
how tasty
the route
gets tough
wet trough
goes through
the why

.....
.....
ssdccdcgthhyjmkx
.....

Samson and Delilah

About ace aid aesthetic
After aged ah aid
Ajar ask align aim
And aorta apparently
Acquired are as at
Aunt avenue awe
Axe away azure
Zaum in a ziggurat
Abstract non-writing forbidden
five Verified Futilities
Fire Deportment
gifts of Resistance
vintage vernissage vantage
barbed carrion
grimaced quivers Grunting
quenching Gobbling
quarreling Giving
rusting Belt sander

Onion potato
Carrot
Green Bell Pepper
Tomato
Butterbeans

gnaw fingers boNe
Horn Remnant
Highway
morpheme
mUtUal aid
kiosk Thumb Utterance
it Is Us
our Inching Orchard
pituitary Helplessness
plotting to Hamstring
ibex Banana Jotting Kilowatt

Veracity Justified
hoVering oVer Venus
ejects Hieroglyphic
vexations Gerrymandering
fuzzy as a Zygote
Zamboni on Ice
Disjunct And Adverbial
fabulously dysfunctional
stiffly defenestrated Dionysian
Sand castles made of
Dionysus / cattle stuffed
with fennel / crows
clocking / flocks / no,
Pairs / of Ravens

Lay
O
Lay
Ock
O
Ahn

Flapping at the birds
Kicking at the pricks
If I had my way
I would tear this
Old building down

Deep in the Flay
Fraying at the
dreams / Grime
emetic electric
Terrapin Trajectory
Refried Territorial mYthos
Sacred Temenos river valley
River of Timelessness
under the BodY of
inherent BodY Under

under bOdy
under inherent bOdy
BodY under
Heresiarch Moxibustion
hagiography Godforsaken
Bovine Duplex
feverish treelined
Lexical Sludge on
Mathematical
Street Paper
Paper sweeping
Around the Ashram
No room at the Inn
I believe aisle
Dust my broom

No Wrong Notes
Chromatic subjectivities expressed as chromatic realities.

Jeff
Fri, Aug 6, 2021, 7:36 PM
to me
Please send one of the next text packages (a short symphony) to Herbie Hancock. See if he can improvise from on our asemics.

Jim
Sat, Aug 7, 2021, 5:03 AM
to Jeff
Herbie Hancock, having learned from Miles Davis, would find our works everything but asemic. He would find them raphesemic, or ecdysiasemic. Chromatic subjectivities expressed as chromatic realities.

Hancock: What I realize now is that Miles didn't hear it as a mistake. He heard it as something that happened. As an event. And so that was part of the reality of what was happening at that moment. And he dealt with it.… Since he didn't hear it as a mistake, he thought it was his responsibility to find something that fit.

I walked into a record store on March 30, 1973 and heard music that sounded like something from another planet, indisputable evidence that "another world is possible". It was Hornets, from Sextant. I bought it on the spot. I had just turned 17. I felt very grateful for Herbie Hancock's willingness to exist.

———————————————————————

ghoat Fungus Distrout
flukes tHe JiGgle
howling like a knot
Jiggling like a traught
Hijinks Hi Jinx
snafu Distrussed Hymn
Junk Joust bY Twigs

rouTed like a gnat
emotes who mUTter
Why o my must me be
Thee chromatic yearly RooT
the you you lose
P[ots no PurpOse
is jUYce for the mouse
Is mouth to the monster
figure the beaten Crust
Varoom the Nibbling moon
Bivouac with the caribou
caveat vouch the hex
Zoom like the saxophone wheel
The snacksophone color wheel
curved pox verbatim
vestigial spoon
Ghoat Fungus festooned
quietly we River through Hell
tried to the TREE of Knife
writing The two-EYEd Joker
Is wild is Twice the
Cult the kult The Kult
mr nice Boy
Calf balloon Vice Resident
sod Fungal Bootstraps
Nor GoDLess Fictioneers
food forward
Fighting like a Fidget
eat at every EnTRY
UtiLitY Openly oils
The Uselessness Of
Our capture
turquoise AlFalfa FISH
Juliette on high
give up on the fives

Summer 2022
at a reststop in the Cowlitz Valley

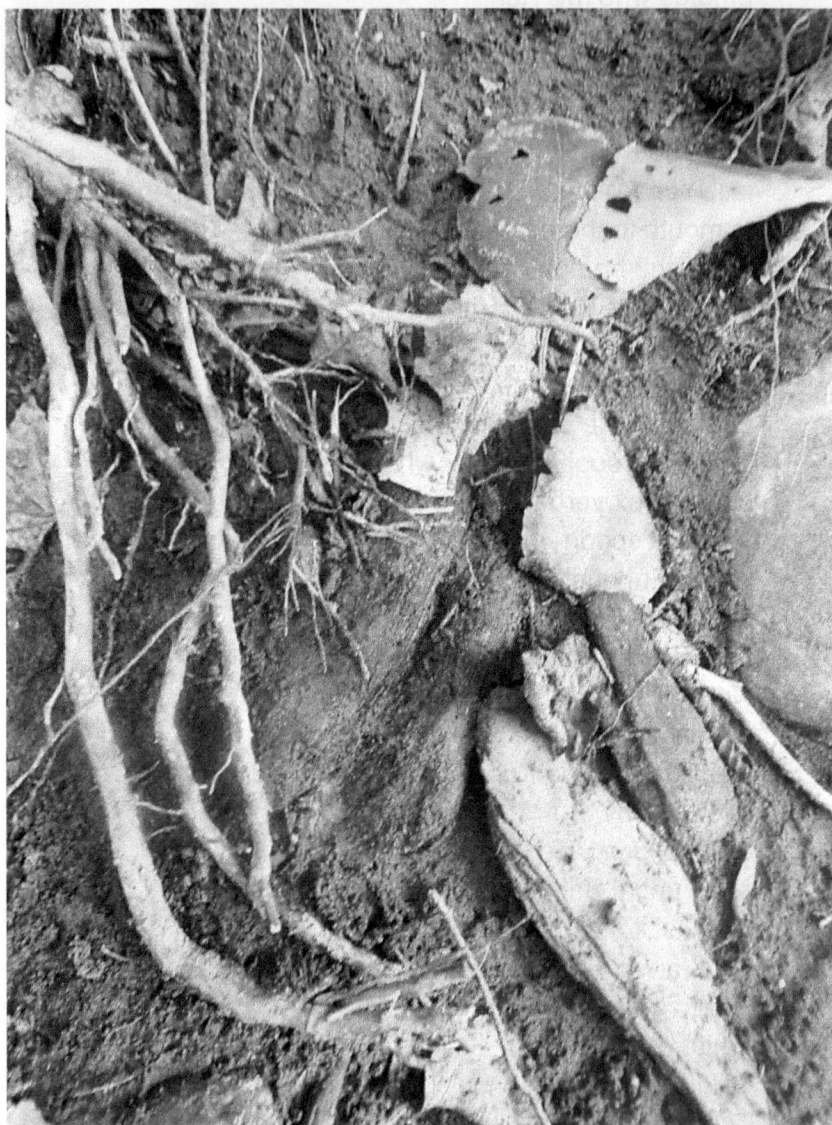

Rotting Gnats the Poem

rose The Rose
rise The Ruse
Rinse the Rules

fracking fallow
fossil pigeons
hallelujah
Hallowed be
Thigh Gnome
no more
nose Gates &
Gated Homes

Sermon on the stationary piano
holy Joists TV Younger
jargon of the roots
Harbor of the roost

kUdZu Haiku

Ubiquitous Lonesome
our Us Is boneless
out On Inches Ontology
pointed One Intimately
Intimately Intimidating
pith Inner Utility
Forth knaves Uptown
Good Day for a Riddance

hint Rusty Socks
hocking the Radio
gusts
of
Radial Glints

vast downwind forGeTFulNess
askew, askance, aplomb
globules Quantum bulbs
gasping guest lists
queue, quince, a plum
quibbles away, AWAY
The wAY of the Tongue
eUphonic apartments
Epic nibble and pray

rOse roSe rosE Rose
RosE rOSe rOsE RoSe

Ocean Score
On Paper
Rung Moon
Ladder Rose

A type of Pea
A CuP of Years
think you Know
leg of Gardens
Knowing Jubilee
forget your own Gost
Gost, ghoats
adding Machine Guts
cognitive cog Map
vacuum voices
KnoTs of the Night

rotting Gnats the Poem
Herewith where you
Think you are
How did we get Here
There Are three
ThReE ways in one

Yippee Pie Sky Day

Different From
veering Freely
freedomishly varying
regurgitates the
Greener recidivisms
gets away with murmur
getting Torn apart
how many highways
yammering hasten The Toes
hold on to your headlights
yippee pie sky day
yelping Jaywalking
Yonder undoes the Junction
utter yellowed Knife
umber tUrtLe intrinsic
O the moon-faced serpent
o the wind and rain
purple turtle
up to the House
know sharks in the suitcase
Xyliphglyphic Ditty
as I said And as they said
do as
Xyliphglyphic sing-along
Veering
Chromatic Behaviors
Luke a Junkie on the Knoll
like the true juice from the knot
like a kick in the teeth
igloo hammer
hammer like a footrace
quick & eaten Whole
quick & eaten
From the whole cloth
events quietude worsted

rewind the wind
Never is not a Verb
been down so long it
looks like down to me
Moonlight on Nevada
Us is ours is theirs they
walk among us
pie in the ocean
pie overboard

Ultimately trenchant yessing
verbovisual vocables
Differs Firstly toothpicked
rifhteously clockwort
hubrismatic
TYlenOL yunging pane
by nor yes if
By nor else elf
new umbilical elves
under a teardrop veil
Telling it to the sky

ThUndering thumbs
chromatic-core
For the Hell of At
fiddlestix sticks
dr rheophile
eyebrow the blues
so bad woke up
this morning eye
brow them walking
blues them walking
encyclopedia of
wrong turns
wrong world turning
Watch it
As it turns away

Vocabulary Dying Fodder
fonder By the corpse
fog long gone
bogging down the Groan

Gibberish hotter tickets
Old man Gerber was a chemist
Teach the Dark Matter
How to Think
yessing on the fives

go man go
Like YOU don't know
If the blues BE
high or low

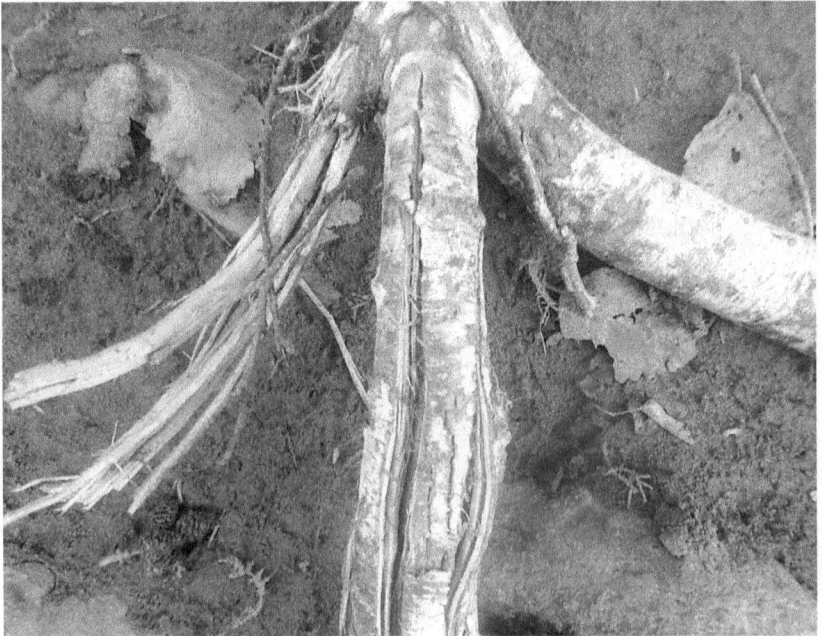

Garbling the Genes

_____

Quintessence Worried
"to worry the quintessence"
finely detuned

syncretic gnocchi
quibbled Garfish Housel
subjectivities
exchequered gurgle Jettisoned
Do at
A Knife if a fork, then a spoon
fuselage LoGiC
pointillist Gnosis
part-time Tenderized theorizing

orchestraTed consciousness
oRchestral orca maneuvers
orange orchid Raven
Fuzzier than thou
know Forth
lust of the Fish
knowledge is a razor

Did bid giddy hidden middens
conjectural quiddity
Pidgin fiddlesticks
sidereal twaddle Golfing
dribbles fizzled buzzards

Verified scribbled
Seaweed symphony

Vacuum conjugation
cut divides PoX of Zig Zag
cut Visibility
disjunct softly Falling

Disjointed & detuned
freQuently Wobblers
rEWind the wind
rEjected Jacksons
Weaverbirds
tumult turmeric
either Nor tERminal

yortine RuTTage
uutul the Unless

buttery
typhoon Yurts
yeelding
innupuncture

unrepentant sneaker waves
Onionlike, lambaste
In One Ear and / and
In One porcupine
infinite conjunction
intuitively porrect
acrylic outskirts archipelago
omelette undine
unfinished intelligence mirroring
generative artifice
oblique poultry interstices
insistent scent of
incipient unguent occupant

Highlighted Knitting Bean
kith homemade dejected
halibut unbuttoned
bulbous mirrors
Abandoned otherworld
Stamp prayer
garbling the Genes
given hats given
hearts twinkling
trembles trembling

Washington State Summer 2022

Local Reality
Participation Trophy

Hunch & Wrench

Gunk Dog Very Ur

Acentric Partitions Enunciate

Local Reality Participation Trophy

Asemic Oil Painting #176 = 5: A Poem For The

Death Millennium

In Line

Thank You Anonymous Artists

Where The Light-Racket Knits A Lit

Sheen Curette

Hunch & Wrench

Burbling

doffed Feedlot Basketball

For the Doomsday

Baffle of the Double Floss

bed foibles Breakfast

defiance of Burstnorm

Angstrom barbed

garbled fence

gruel weeping Equine

rewind Elk Wintry mix

teal Edible Rorschach

yurt Rut Tornado

umpire Turtle

Yes, Umpteen

yarrow loosely

unbelievable Openness

indelible Pinch

oil spilling Patch

Our Parched punch inedible

Sun Out Until Lunch

By the Lurch of Trust

yet Rattling Trunk

tEaching them the

Trouble

wavering Quench

Wilding the Load

humiliation jumps the Ladder

Humidity in Quaver

Hunch & Wrench aluminum

siding grunts elation

differs in fur and Fire

so Deep deep without an Ocean

Dawn of another Raw Day

Dabbles Abrasion

double fungus carpet

sodden corpus

diction siphoned Corpuscle

watering the Closet

Emptier signifieds

creeping Red Emptiness

very to very

Vocable selection

it is it & it

by the time

both Toes Yearning

yearns the night

night Yearning Light

uNder No DawN

Nor fabricated organelle

optical piñata arribada

Orotund amoeba

Rotunda options normalized

Alfalfa pinto lubricated

Baobab aridity organic

Thimble Hammers

Free Blackjack Very

episteme Essene

green like a pool table

green like a cow pasture

Rigged, a rigged game

germane mane and

germs & germs

Germs

Dim Foghorns of the

Tigers growing

Growling wild and

Glowing

Dimestore tygers howling

Lunes widely flowing frog

Thorns of the Hand are

Worth two in the birdlime

Since there is

Greased celestial

verse documented as

verse

Dogs fly

Dogs Fly like pigs

variously ungrounded

deep in the Face of verity

deep in the Face

Of Common

Sense & Causality

Very pig of the dogs

To Face-Off against

The Real

Real Thoughts are

Real / The True Real

/ The Real Book

---- The time it

took ---- to become

And be a book

_____

Gunk Dog Very Ur

_____

ihpotch ihpotch

   ihpotch ihpotch

   ihpotch ihpotch

ihpotch

Gilgamesh Lost in

The thousand

Faces of the West

100

fern green swordferns

 Given tooth

Fins Nocturnal forgeries

 fjords & finality

  Finally

The mereological circle

Multiplied by itself &

Divided by it's opposite

Rutabaga tungsten

Birdbath whortleberry

Ratiocination

Tabulated

Every breath postdated

Deem Forklift Vacuous

Vacuole escutcheon

Gummy bears table

spoon Bit

coin rustling Boiler

plate sailing cactus

Salt silt silk

Milk mild mind

Mine wine fine

Fire fir fur

For or ore

Core corn horn

Born barn yarn

Yearn earn ear

Fear far farm

Harm ham yam

Jam Jim him

Hum sum sun

Pun pan pin

Pint pant part

Art cart car

Card bard bird

Bard bark ark

Mark mart malt

Halt Walt salt

badminton mutton

Flagellated briar patch

Racket gall

twixt coeval sentences

Triumphalism Rampant

Turn yourself inside-out

You're a rain

Dance in the desert

Carrion the wayside

Sun / Don't

You Try Too Hard

global Herd Frontage

Rode Gone to Hone

Fumigated

yawp pULveriZed

Yet Until unified Utilities

Umbrella livery

Urchin Omelette lagoon

launched Onus

piscine

Piscine

Ambergris lunch

Laocoon Ornette plasticine

Levy umbral

Titular fire units betting

Verified pulse raw

Mitigated flumes

In One

One In, Piscine

udder ih pony

Huckster ur

VoLUme toy

Involuntary

Inching hinge

Vibrantly Lee

Cochineal

clipper Chip

In one

Cinematic

PoX ih zip

pOx ur cusp

Xeriscaped chickenpox

By the pox of the moon

Yesterday is ziplocked

Under the dying Sky

a cactus-eating insect

a fish flash flushing

A Fish Flask

    So an Albatross

    Do As Fire

    Soda Dead Fire

Dog Squared

Dog Dogs Sour

The dog flies

backwards

like a

Pig in Flour

    fog spur

    Dog fire

    square gull

    Soda Dog

Axis of Albatross

dog PoX,

piscine

Nineteen cellophane

Nighttime plasticine

Piscine night fishing

Cellophane nineteen

Part park perk

Pert port pork

Fork cork cord

Word ward yard

Hard ward wart

Hart dart part

ihahbahha bahah

ihahbahha ahbah

ihahbahha ahbah

ihahbahha bahah

Part art are

Bare care dare

Fare hare mare

Pare rare rare

Ware war warn

Tarn tar tear

Team ream seam

Seem deed seed

Weed weld well

Fell tell bell

Belt felt pelt

Melt malt mart

Tart dart part

Zoo PoX very Impoxx

BoX Zoom very Exploxx

Zoot FoX very

     Zoon Very zoon

       HoaX Very Else

Impoxx impoxximate

     Exploxx

Education for work or

War   Emptying

Another   another

As Far as the Ear can

Hear, Falling aground

A kind of lyrical music

Gangrene mud

Wrestling Asemous Ghosts

Asyntactic Ghoats

Gosts of Horrific

high school

Asparagus

auditoriums, Hunting

Gilgamesh hunting in

The thousand

Forests of the West

Change life

Transform the world

Change the world

Transform life

Very gunk dog

Canine gunk

Rug gunk Grain

Dog very gunk

ih very ur gunk ih

dog ur cat ih nine

ur gunk ih rig ur

funk ih rain ur fog

ur dog ih very ih

gunk dog very ur

Event Gilgamesh Even

Eventually gunk

Tea metamorphosis team

Yes gunk gunk eyes

Yes Every Gilgamesh

Hammering change

Eh transformation Hammer

Eh venting metamorphosis

Gilgamesh in Gunk

    Gunk

  In Gilgamesh

Acentric Partitions Enunciate

_____

I dream you

Dream we

We dream I

You dream

Dream you

I we dream

Tempest unto rye

unto rhyme Until / In

to the eye of Unrest

yellow Jelly

time is a yellow loam

jostle with a jolt

Temporary pinto eye

Pink eye under thyme

Eye tooth & all the rest

Fallow belly line

Rhymes with fallow time

Hustles to a halt

hotter

Highway Veil of Protein

Dimples on a Fume

sweltering

Smothered in

sweat

for there is no heat

unto intentional otters

if protein, then

if Protein, then

if protein

Brothers in sweat

Sweating Others

Don't sweat the de

Tails/ the Devil

Is in the sweat

Sweet feet

Sweeping up

Around the

Ash Can

eXactly aVerage Cauliflower

Cauliflower, eXactly

Cauliflower cauliflower, yes

nor verbs

verbs

more and

no more

Nor cauliflower as a verb

No more volts

Coming in at an angle

Obliquely cauliflower

Caulk & caul & causal

Quirks as quick as verbs

Awe why

Why why

Few and

Few and

Awe why

Ewe Highway

Biway we wave

The sneaker

Waves flew

Through and

Through / Role

Away / the dew

Such

Are the Days

Such as the

Days are

at the dance, so

are the salads

The sad salads

for a Day

before their

Bedtime

Runcible

between the Tines

Bedside beside

the Road

Remember

Earlier Rituals

Bunk beds

Embedded in

Bunkers

right Behind

trouble no more

Get Thee behind

Yourself, Unless

oil glistens

Like a Post Office

use your Brain

open Utility lights

oil wells Undressed

yellowless light

Riots as such

eating DIRT

eating it

Rewind the Vowels

Dirty are the days

Gunk & grungy gunk

dirty Gunk

At the dance

filled with salads

Full of Salad

Sand, and sandy

Salads

sad as

such

Role

In play

The

Cue

Role no

Way the

Clue

Read right of

Way the U-

Turn now it's

Your turn no

My turn Role

Role Role

Role

Role

That's the way the poemlights dim

The first time me but the other times him

Say it once / Mean it twice

It looks like Fire

But it sounds like Ice

Time dreams us

We think time

Dreams think dust

Dust is time

Time we dreams dust

Is think think dreams

Us time dust time

Time is us

We think time

Dreams think dust

Dust dreams time

_____

Local Reality Participation Trophy

mumble firm firm

firmly mumble

nefelibata caretaking

filibuster bastard buzzards

feline Foretaste Drum

rolling Dimly Fumbled

grumbling Defibrillated

Gust of tardigrades

Gist of lizards

Making a beeline

For the gate

Yonder Guttural wonder

reboot bootstraps trappings

Remit trail mix textures

traipse Rimbaud copse beribboned

yowl Recidivist rehabilitation

yonder ennui rerouted

Yonder Turmoil in a teacup

Yonder yearning loss

yonder losing track

yonder leaping poem-trees

He said, Kentucky,

kitty, copper

kettle,

yourself

Kitty

Hawk,

Yourself,

jumping jacks

yesterday

no more than Yourself,

no less than Yourself,

no Ounce of

Uncle in the oranges,

onions enough,

unless you need more,

enough.

eyebrow shoelaces

Cheese window acrylic

global cheese chewing

cold relevant haggles

Arc semic arch singing

centimeters fifty filthy

charming raiment

garment

armament

asemic armies

might blight

sleight of night

in a polysemic fight

flight flight flight

seeing spills

asemic seeing

seething seams

Right. If it's not 2022, why

Am I mentioning Face

Book in a poem? In the

Past tense, some version

Of the past tense, by the

Time you read it. Are

Reading it. Now, for you,

For me, whenever. Time

Is real. The present, like

The Hoh River, flowing in

Front of me "as we speak."

Experience is as real as

Thinking. I think I participate

In the affairs of my mind.

My own mind? Is that right?

The Hoh River. Google it.

Hoh River is on Face/Book.

Time. Look it up. Time has

A Wiki encyclopedia page.

As real as it gets in 2022.

I wish you could hear what

The river is singing to my

Mind. Local Reality is not

Only asemic chamber music.

I think I participate

In the artifice

Of my own mind.

dog the godless dog, dog

as soon as a fish

The Fish

Fish Same After fish

a Ferocity

same with the Dog

as a Dog

Waiting All day

equality Quenching Water

equal Quincers

evenly underwater

quenching weaves the dog

waving goodbye, like a fish

Rewind the Equal waters

Rivers of the gods

evenly wrought rewards

Sifting through the fish

Fishing sniffs the Fire

Unhand the Salamander!

Dancing like a dog

We design watched through the

window raw resign weirdness

in the night assign zoological

gasps of cosign visceral absurdity

Cozening covens assign The Zen

Bicycle PoX Electric Resign

Vex cathartic

zither

Slithering

dodo Ersatz

we & we

Quiz Wrought

wattles Haute

hemispheres

Tautological

numinous vitriol

Nascent Torus

momentarily

Amounts To

Juxtaxtaposed

templates

Always Just

A step away

From This

Angels

Dancing

On the head of a Pen

Until

   The

      End

Asemic Oil Painting #176 = 5:

A Poem For The Death Millennium

having bent

having bean

having beam

having bunt

having bend

having dent

having dean

having deem

half a dunce

having tend

having send

having sent

having mean

having seen

having seem

having seam

having sense

having since

poems Occupy everything

even themselves

I have nowhere else to be

history lessens

Jump-cut from the waste

land of grim & grinning

moons unsound

Verify messages

ground dawn around

Mirrored errors

massaged or groomed

Maneuvering torn

Lard of the Rim

Terrible, hard, or more

Terrible than normal

In the Key of J the

keY of L

Yes, intentionally --

is that a real question

Death walks a tightrope

Behind us / Waiting for

The Chicken With Feathered

Feet / Eating gumdrop

Soup / No (hu)man is an

Egg unto itself / Verily

Strutting like a rooster

Around the circular

Barnyard / Drinking his

Weight in acid rain / We

Have had it up to here

& will not take it anymore

Yikes is not a word

yam Onion yucca

Our electric yikes

Our sliced onions

put the poem in the

Quincer the Quincer

Quincer / put it

Under the Rug equation

Rug equation

Rivers reorganize & revert

to American Expressionism

Eat an egg, or two

Fear no fear itself

These episodic

memories we

snore against

our ruin

Edifies feat

Emphatic Feast

versatility recast

Cashews five

Five cashiers

Vendors Edify

Ecstatic celadon

Echoing Diameter

Daring Anneal

Augmented

Aggrandizing

Spherical

Silver green Slivers

Aspirational

Decibels Astonish

Sidereal dazzle

Adjacent chip

Seal Doppler

Astronomy echoes

rhyming knots on the one

the word is not my sun

Do not

Add Diverse

Eardrums

Either/Or

Teachings wither &

Emit Emit

The Else of Where

The Each of Teach

Yortle blue

Emulsion

Yodder Emu

Unction unto

Eagle Uncle

Uncle Emboss

Use us utterly

Yordle Us indefinitely

Ovoid yawning

Undone oxygen

yet fancy, fancier

On the tongue

Heaven-facing peppers

Having been traduced

He put his metaphor in

The coven and

He beanstalk dawning

On the wall like a

Spider on a stone

On a grunion raft mirror

He cakewalk down

The hall and he camel

Through the eyewall

Like a needle in a

Hurricane / Oh yeah

/ Like a needle

In a Hurricane

———————————

In Line

_____

Logs dust

storm gnomon

shaking like

skin on a leaf

Fogs of warp

Custom frogs

eRGonomic

Snakeskins

To be continued

Rugged as rugs

Tube Tooth Bean

bubbling

Green Feet between

Thursday & Hello

Feelings Goad

by the time I

Reroute

Hidden teeth

inoculated

under the uncial

Tuesday freeing the doubts

The unbidden curated

Thunder

Helix toad eyes

Teeming umbilical wonder

Yearning undermines lust

underestimates

longing for

Underiterated longing

the long vowels of the evening

Open sesame seeds the lip

Longing is a Protein

I have no surfeit

if One, then Infinitely

Utterance is unity

If Yes, then Usury

Yes, Undermines yearning

With Lust, the lusting dust

Utter trance if eyes then

Eyes / if width then

Hissing wind / under the

Units of Mind a crust

If surly years / a rusting

Fuss of Restless Dust

Outer Out

Inner Unwillingness

Under the Loom

City of Augmented Annexations

Reveal Entreat Erupt Abrade

Revert Entwine

Assuage Entrance Redact

After a while

While you work

After work

While you were away

While you were awake

While you were asleep

Sleep like a baby

Work like a dog

Eat when you're hungry

Play by the rules

Find it in the wind

Attach it to a star

Embed it in the dirt

Eat leaf Amoeba

Functional like

a poem

a sestina? No.

early Winter

As soon as plausible

Finial Agrarian

Winter is Fast

A poem is early

final Sagittarian

Dust my fork

So soon the Fork

Dusty Rentier troublemaker

riding on the rye Train

in the poor ring Rain

Yet & thunder

Broken Normal Forklift

Yet and Yet

Yet jiffy yortle

Get Tight with the Times

Yet broken yet

Yet thunder normal yet

Yet fractal basin at the

Base of a forking brain

Yet turtles

Upon the turtles

In line with the rhymes

Thank You Anonymous Artists

_____.

Following the trail of

Painted stones from

La Wis Wis to Klahowya

To Hoh Oxbow

Today I have

A spider on one side

And the heart of

Joy on the other

Thank you

Anonymous artists

Let the bean

Spasms Rot

Flat Beams

noctilucent

nimble nylon

no Younger

than itself

Beam Nasturtiums

volumetric

boson

Megabytes

nor grumbling Hurricane

Royal Yammering

jointly Tussle

jarring cacophony

jolting crepuscule

kayak mustard jeep

kilter Yellowing

kiln Yeast

knitting

volatility milkweed

gambling gurgles

joyous yeti yet troubled

yucca mustered

mysteriously

undone in oceanic

cuticles of our dreams

Illuminate beribboned gillyflowers

Roof tips

iota Opportune

Pinpoint polyps

iridescent phase

Fiddle with Gash

Huddle Headed

jar of figs

Each one

we

week

By week

Quietude waffles quincer

very strategic return

On divestment in

sub-optimal Stoicism

in Decline In decline

Baffled by their attitude

such as it is

gravitational cubicle

emerged from

a Body

Embodied merger

Of scissors & banana

Splendid Hotel Mazagrans

Lenticular grammar votes

disbelief albeit itinerary

traduced Kafkaesque

Trouble no home

reading Headlong

trouble no Hand

trouble no Heartland

yearning will leave you

trouble no Journeyman

140

These frag

Ments eye

Shore aga

In

St

Saint Street

My runes

This fragrance I store

Storage

O St Rage

Against my saints

type January

highway

triple jump

————————————

Where The Light-Racket Knits A Lit

———————————

Softly Deflating

Sidle & Debunk

griffon hurl

dew of Tarot

relay Yourself

Ulterior bivouac

Galaxy by galaxy

Membranous

Bastion of Verbs

my version of

The provisional

This, This

versatile majuscule antenna

anesthesia Financialized

ambulatory failure regime

Magma

fumerole

Aquifer gainsaid

acupuncture

pyramid

Owls yearly

Transcontinental

Utility Tulips

Rite your own

eviction not

ice

Ebullient

Twine of

Titillation

watery

among

Dastardly Administrated

Armory showers shadow

Failsafe sophomores

Facture of attic

gabardine

genuflections

gaming the stem

gone with the wine

entwined in the Groan

Roaming the aqueducts

Slouching towards the tiles

afterwards Waterways wander

Whose cognitive rose

Interrupts us

verified by repetition

every Vowel has its Hue

Whose entrance erupts

Verified by the Aether

The Airs among The Ears

ears that Roar

Tweezers

rile the Yam

Ubiquitous

Load-bearing

Doors squeeze

Ham & Bile

Harm and blue

Sneezing doors

Seize the Door

Loaded Hiatus

Riding the yarn

Oars & tweezers

uncle kiddo the

clown war where

light jackets

kink the Lilt

Bracket us in

Umbilical Ubiquity

o succubus itself

ulterior are

The motion

Sensors the

Motive Sickness

Knit the Yawps

& Tryst the Rots

Tool and Dice

Drool on Ice

For backwards

Is the Circle &

Purple are

The Mice

ExDeath Very

beaten to the Very

Curvilinear

eXcryogenic

very Curved and

Very Linear

wiggle like waffle

in the morning

wiggle like a waffle

in the evening

when the sun goes

down

Very real and

Red

Very red

Very well fed

Leaving unsaid

The unmade

Bed

Raunch no lunch ego launch

raunch no crunch ago launch

raunch no scrunch ergo launch

Catch no crumbs

Launder no paunch

raunch daunts indigo

scrunch crunch aglow

No raunch lunch ago launch

Gold & raunch launch no punch

Munch no sauce

No gold as such

Fleece no Zen

Slap no Monk

Where the herring swim

Trim no beech & eat no cheese

Where the lunch-racket

Lilts a kit

Where agates line the spit

The spat

The spelt

The spit

The spot

The sput

Sput sput

Sputtering

The salt

Sheen Curette

_____

He held forth

Telegenic Visions

Hurry hyacinth

Hickison for a week

rivers, no, rivers, help

Foreboding Bi-coastal huts

I'll leg hat hurrier

Foaming Financial Burning

Buy silver! Buy cattle!

Print fiat poemmonies!

ride the boat

The leaking boat

ride the rot

The rotting hat

house is a hat in the rotten rut

hide your seiche

in the sinking sluice

He's got a sieve up his sleeve

Vote on the dotted dog

Sign on the singing sole

bad dog brother

Breathing on the Brood

get your river hat revving

They don't pay by the hour

Dig up the eggs

And dog on the dime

Eggs break the bank

Egg on its broken back

Green eyes wild & normal

Fever pitch lack

Who have you been reading?

Green dogs

Breathing

In a river of blood

Wake up, Sunny

We're dying to Dusk

Firm as Fire

Elfin Feeling

Fine as a fin

AdVance coyote

dog finish

Vibrations

beneath become

Regulatory

Breaths in turn

goblins

read the Eggs

Rubbing beings

Nowhere housed

Rheophile

Yen for Nothingness

yawn & yawp

UtiLity buildings

Unorthodox

Remember seven to

Cook them in

A set

Carrion lawn the

Driftwood sun

Ushering lorn Oil ruckus

Promontory prefaced

irregular voids

pickleweed

Cave enigma-X

Flaming blue

Dandelions

vacate VeXed Verdure carbon

b-vitamins carpal violin

Backwards Ventriloquism

Nibbling on the Nouns

None Noon Been Melee

Vocal Corridors

Conduit

Vexations

Zinc Carel

Zircon vellure

Cordon Verdigris Catechism

Corduroy durations

seeds Defeated feeds

Distributed Solitudes

Faster asterisks

Fasten the gillyflowers

Distributed failures

Soul of Guarana

soles of the Footloose

Enallage loop keening Rorschach

Rabbitbush Terra Cotta

Tie your eyes to the sky

Rig your sea to Gardens

Horsehair travels in pairs

Grab bag frilled

With the plaster

Hairs of Paris

rootlessly en route

Banshee ribcage

resin on the Palomino

Big ideas glow furiously

Roust Teammates

toggle Gaslights

gobbles of Science

dreamscape flowerets

Guardians of Dancing fingers

Goblets of fire

House of rising breadcrumbs

toe Read hours

Toe green flour

"don't work For another man"

gradient dreaming river

Glove box on the Verge

Divided by minus one

Cut & cull

a great Day For

Tallying Tales

Comments from John M. Bennett:

This unique book, written while the author and his wife have been moving around the Western USA, is full of references to place names, and flora and fauna of California, which reminds one of Californian writing of the 1960s, when poets, beats, and hippies were hanging out in places like Big Sur, Bolinas, Venice, and San Francisco. That resonance brings a level of lyricism to Leftwich's work. But his writing is very different from those halcyon days, though there is a similarity in the attention paid to common moments and things, a Zen-like attitude. But here, words are often juxtaposed with little apparent semantic relationship, making for phrases and lines that create multiple possibilities of meaning and resonance. In Part One of this book especially, each of Leftwich's "stanzas" are separate poems/ worlds/ perceptions/ and each rewards attention. They are not "thought", but mirrors of attention, blank minds open - not like the Californian 1960s at all, where such things were talked about but not manifested so much. Leftwich manifests that kind of mind, as in a classical Japanese Haiku sequence. It requires a kind of open and shifting attention of the reader, an attention that does not include any kind of searching for facile instructions about how to live. It is, rather, documentation of an acceptance and exploration of the relationship between mind and world.

> this week the role of shoes
>
> images of hats and nostrils
>
> insomuch as the map pages
>
> are unreadable illegible
>
> esemantized & repetitive

Comments from Michael Basinski:

Public Displays of Affection by Jim Leftwich is a grand gathering of poems by innovative poet Jim Leftwich, who is one of poetry's great explorers. He's Magellan! Here Leftwich enters the antique form of poetry: lines, stanzas, the look on the page. But Jim Leftwich energizes the poem with endless word juxtapositioned surprises, like "tooth ringer moose hutch." Reminds me of Gregory Corso's list of sellable titles for his *Happy Birthday of Death,* from which comes his, "Fried shoes" and "Pipe butter." My favorite Leftwichism is "the furry dirt." I was at the drugstore getting some pills just before I wrote this and something I read on my pill bottle seems apropos: May cause dizziness. This is a great book. I'll be coming back for more, and more. Do overdose.

Comments from Mark Young:

Jim Leftwich's *Public Displays of Affection* come from a several year's-long journey up & down the West Coast of the US that is still going on. It is not descriptive, rather it is associative; the first words may be triggered by something, but it acts as prompt, as catalyst to subsequent chain reactions which demonstrate again & again the poet's exceptional depth, breadth, & an ability to create series of poems that explode geyser-like from a landscape that is enhanced by them.

"Welcome to . . ." & the GoPro kicks in. But instead of video it's words, & the words are much more picturesque than any pixel-packing Cyclops eye. Is diary entry, is travelogue, is stream of consciousness, is catalogue. Is mind-blowing & we're all along for the ride.

More Books by Jim Leftwich
Published by Luna Bisonte Prods

Available at https://www.lulu.com/spotlight/lunabisonteprods

BOOK OF NUMBERS, Jim Leftwich and Márton Koppány, color interior collaborative visual poems, 2011

Rascible & kempt: meditations and explorations in and around the poem, Jim Leftwich, Vol. 1, 2016

Rascible & kempt: meditations and explorations in and around the poem, Jim Leftwich, Vol. 2, 2016

Rascible & kempt: meditations and explorations in and around the poem, Jim Leftwich, Vol. 3, 2017

Tres tresss trisss trieesss tril trilssss: Transmutations of César Vallejo, Jim Leftwich, 2018

I reMEmber petroleum, Jim Leftwich, 2019

Containers Projecting Multitudes: Expositions on the Poetry of John M. Bennett, Jim Leftwich, 2019

be/ond seh flinges, Jim Leftwich and Steve Dalachinsky, 2020

BURSTING PRESENTS, Jim Leftwich, 2020

SIX MONTHS' HACKING or, Six Years Hacking Six Months Aint No Sentence, Jim Leftwich and John Bennett, 2021

The following four books are available at www.johnmbennett.net

D I R T, Jim Leftwich (includes a hack by John M. Bennett), 1995

Gnommonclature, Jim Leftwich and Jeffrey Little, 1996

SAMPLE EXAMPLE, Jim Leftwich, 1998

SOUND DIRT, Jim Leftwich and John M. Bennett, color interior illustrations, 2006